AAT

AQ2016

ADVANCED DIPLOMA IN ACCOUNTING

Spreadsheets for Accounting

EXAM KIT

This Exam Kit supports study for the following AAT qualifications:
AAT Advanced Diploma in Accounting – Level 3
AAT Advanced Certificate in Bookkeeping – Level 3
AAT Advanced Diploma in Accounting at SCQF – Level 6

British Library Cataloguing-in-Publication Data

A catalogue record for this book is available from the British Library.

Published by:

Kaplan Publishing UK

Unit 2 The Business Centre

Molly Millar's Lane

Wokingham

Berkshire

RG41 2QZ

ISBN: 978-1-83996-090-1

© Kaplan Financial Limited, 2021

Printed and bound in Great Britain.

The text in this material and any others made available by any Kaplan Group company does not amount to advice on a particular matter and should not be taken as such. No reliance should be placed on the content as the basis for any investment or other decision or in connection with any advice given to third parties. Please consult your appropriate professional adviser as necessary. Kaplan Publishing Limited and all other Kaplan group companies expressly disclaim all liability to any person in respect of any losses or other claims, whether direct, indirect, incidental, consequential or otherwise arising in relation to the use of such materials.

All rights reserved. No part of this examination may be reproduced or transmitted in any form or by any means, electronic or mechanical, including photocopying, recording, or by any information storage and retrieval system, without prior permission from Kaplan Publishing.

This Product includes content from the International Ethics Standards Board for Accountants (IESBA), published by the International Federation of Accountants (IFAC) in 2015 and is used with permission of IFAC.

CONTENTS

Features in this exam kit

In addition to providing a range of real exam style questions, we have also included in this kit:

- unit-specific information and advice on exam technique

- our recommended approach to make your revision for this particular unit as effective as possible.

You will find a wealth of other resources to help you with your studies on the AAT website:

www.aat.org.uk/

Quality and accuracy are of the utmost importance to us so if you spot an error in any of our products, please send an email to mykaplanreporting@kaplan.com with full details, or follow the link to the feedback form in MyKaplan.

Our Quality Co-ordinator will work with our technical team to verify the error and take action to ensure it is corrected in future editions.

SPREADSHEETS FOR ACCOUNTING

UNIT GUIDE

This Advanced level unit is about using spreadsheets to accurately enter, analyse and present information so that informed accountancy judgements can be made. The skills and knowledge from this unit integrate spreadsheet use within the other Advanced level accountancy subjects.

Accounting technicians need to use spreadsheets as it is important that financial information is accurately analysed and presented in an unambiguous way. Spreadsheets are widely used within industry, commerce and practice, and a variety of spreadsheet packages are available specifically to assist with accounting roles (routine and one-off): Features of spreadsheet packages allow calculations, manipulation of data, analysis, budgeting, preparing financial statements, reporting, forecasting and decision making.

Students must have access to a suitable spreadsheet software package as part of their study for this unit and for the assessment. The program selected by learning providers must be capable of producing reports in the following format at various stages of the process: XLSX. Assessment evidence submitted in alternative file formats will not be marked.

LEARNING OUTCOMES

LO1	Design and structure appropriate spreadsheets to meet customer needs
LO2	Use spreadsheet software to record, format and organise data
LO3	Use relevant tools to manipulate and analyse data
LO4	Use software tools to verify accuracy and protect data
LO5	Use tools and techniques to prepare and report accounting information

FORMAT OF THE ASSESSMENT

The practice assessment comprises five tasks and covers all assessment objectives. Students will be assessed by computer-based assessment. Marking of the assessment is wholly by humans.

In any one assessment, students may not be assessed on all content, or on the full depth or breadth of a piece of content. The content assessed may change over time to ensure validity of assessment, but all assessment criteria will be tested over time.

The following weighting is based upon the AAT Qualification Specification documentation which may be subject to variation.

	Assessment objective	Weighting
LO1	Design and structure appropriate spreadsheets to meet customer needs	5%
LO2	Use spreadsheet software to record, format and organise data	25%
LO3	Use relevant tools to manipulate and analyse data	45%
LO4	Use software tools to verify accuracy and protect data	10%
LO5	Use tools and techniques to prepare and report accounting information	15%
		100%

Time allowed: 2 hours

PASS MARK: The pass mark for all AAT assessments is 70%.

 Always keep your eye on the clock and make sure you attempt all questions!

The detailed syllabus and study guide written by the AAT can be found at:

www.aat.org.uk/

ASSESSMENT INFORMATION FOR STUDENTS

- The assessment is closed book. You must not use any additional support material, other than the workbook provided, to generate your evidence.

- You should read the task scenario and instructions carefully and complete all tasks. It should take you no longer than 2 hours to complete all tasks.

- All work must be submitted for marking within 7 days of the assessment centre unlocking the assessment. Any work not uploaded within this time will not be marked.

- Before submitting your work for marking, you must sign the 'Declaration of authenticity' to confirm that you have not had any help with this assessment. The declaration must also be completed and countersigned by your assessment centre, then submitted with your work. It is important that all work produced is your own. If you fail to confirm authenticity of work produced, your work will not be marked.

- If during the marking process we suspect impersonation, plagiarism, or any other form of malpractice an investigation will be carried out. Sanctions will be imposed, or disciplinary action taken if there is clear evidence that malpractice has taken place.

- Once your work has been submitted to AAT for marking, you must delete the task instructions and your assessment workbook from the PC and/or other equipment (e.g. USB) on which it has been stored. You must not copy or share the task instructions or assessment workbook with anyone else.

INDEX TO QUESTIONS AND ANSWERS

The workbooks and the answers to these scenarios can be found as excel files on your MyKaplan account.

The answers to the tasks in these scenarios can be found as spreadsheet files on your MyKaplan account (together with the text and word files required).

Please go to www.mykaplan.co.uk and login using your username and password

EXAM TECHNIQUE

- **Do not skip any of the material** in the syllabus.

- **Read each question** *very* carefully.

- **Double-check your answer** before committing yourself to it.

- Answer **every** question – if you do not know an answer to a multiple choice question or true/false question, you don't lose anything by guessing. Think carefully before you **guess**.

- If you are answering a multiple-choice question, **eliminate first those answers that you know are wrong.** Then choose the most appropriate answer from those that are left.

- **Don't panic** if you realise you've answered a question incorrectly. Getting one question wrong will not mean the difference between passing and failing.

Computer-based exams – tips

- Do not attempt a CBA until you have **completed all study material** relating to it.

- On the AAT website there is a CBA demonstration. It is **ESSENTIAL** that you attempt this before your real CBA. You will become familiar with how to move around the CBA screens and the way that questions are formatted, increasing your confidence and speed in the actual exam.

- Be sure you understand how to use the **software** before you start the exam. If in doubt, ask the assessment centre staff to explain it to you.

- Questions are **displayed on the screen** and answers are entered using keyboard and mouse. At the end of the exam, in the case of those units not subject to human marking, you are given a certificate showing the result you have achieved.

- In addition to the traditional multiple-choice question type, CBAs will also contain **other types of questions**, such as number entry questions, drag and drop, true/false, pick lists or drop down menus or hybrids of these.

- In some CBAs you will have to type in complete computations or written answers.

- You need to be sure you **know how to answer questions** of this type before you sit the exam, through practice.

KAPLAN'S RECOMMENDED REVISION APPROACH

QUESTION PRACTICE IS THE KEY TO SUCCESS

Success in professional examinations relies upon you acquiring a firm grasp of the required knowledge at the tuition phase. In order to be able to do the questions, knowledge is essential.

However, the difference between success and failure often hinges on your exam technique on the day and making the most of the revision phase of your studies.

The **Kaplan Study Text** is the starting point, designed to provide the underpinning knowledge to tackle all questions. However, in the revision phase, poring over text books is not the answer.

Kaplan Pocket Notes are designed to help you quickly revise a topic area; however you then need to practise questions. There is a need to progress to exam style questions as soon as possible, and to tie your exam technique and technical knowledge together.

The importance of question practice cannot be over-emphasised.

The recommended approach below is designed by expert tutors in the field, in conjunction with their knowledge of the examiner and the specimen assessment.

You need to practise as many questions as possible in the time you have left.

OUR AIM

Our aim is to get you to the stage where you can attempt exam questions confidently, to time, in a closed book environment, with no supplementary help (i.e. to simulate the real examination experience).

Practising your exam technique is also vitally important for you to assess your progress and identify areas of weakness that may need more attention in the final run up to the examination.

In order to achieve this we recognise that initially you may feel the need to practice some questions with open book help.

Good exam technique is vital.

THE KAPLAN REVISION PLAN

Stage 1: Assess areas of strengths and weaknesses

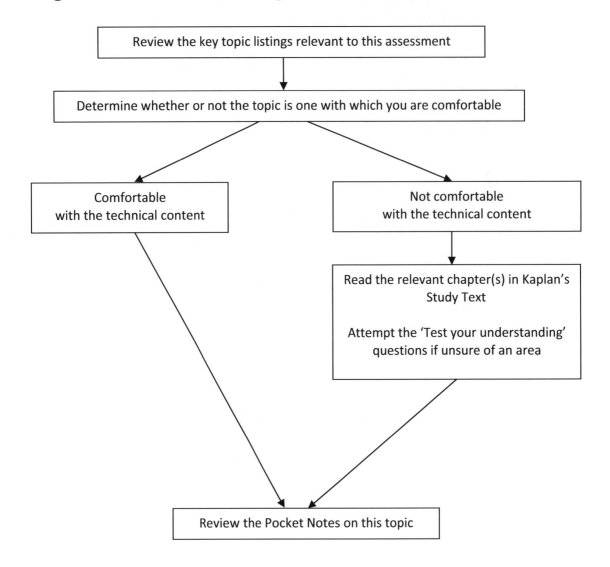

Stage 2: Practice questions

Follow the order of revision of topics as presented in this Kit and attempt the questions in the order suggested.

Try to avoid referring to Study Texts and your notes and the model answer until you have completed your attempt.

Review your attempt with the model answer and assess how much of the answer you achieved.

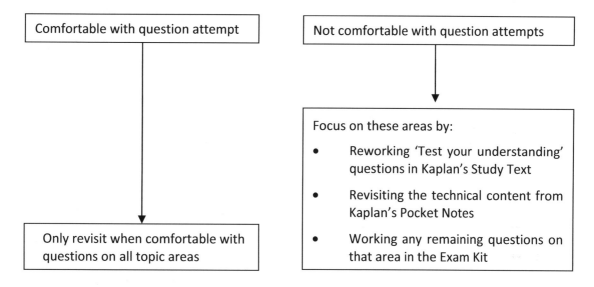

Stage 3: Final pre-exam revision

We recommend that you **attempt at least one mock examination** containing a set of previously unseen exam-standard questions.

Attempt the mock CBA online in timed, closed book conditions to simulate the real exam experience.

SPSH PRACTICE SCENARIOS

The excel workbooks and answers can be within the SPSH course on MyKaplan.

Please go to www.mykaplan.co.uk and login using your username and password.

SCENARIO 1

SLICK PARTZ

You are an Accounting Technician working for the UK Branch of a company called Slick Partz. Your branch is a franchise of the parent company which is based in Europe. Slick Partz manufactures parts for hospital equipment at its factory in main land Europe and these are then sold to franchisees. The franchise is then responsible for selling the parts to hospitals in its sales area.

The franchise buys the parts from the parent company in Euros (€) but sells to the hospitals in GB Pounds (£).

Required:

TASK 1

On 'Sheet 1' worksheet:

(a) In Column D format the Cost Price data as currency. It should be formatted as € Euros (€ 123) to 2 decimal places.

(b) In Columns E and F format the Cost Price and Sale Price data as currency. It should be formatted to GB Pounds to 2 decimal places.

(c) Rename Sheet 1 as 'Data'.

(d) Copy the 'Data' worksheet to a new worksheet in the same workbook and name it as 'Subtotals'.

(e) Go back to the 'Data' worksheet and set the page orientation to portrait and fit the data to the width of one page.

(f) Save the workbook as 'Slick Partz'.

TASK 2

On the 'Subtotals' worksheet:

(a) Sort the data before carrying out subtotalling. The subtotals that are needed are for Model and Salesperson.

(b) Create subtotals for Model, summing the Sales quantity.

(c) Create a further subtotal for Salesperson, summing the Sales quantity.

(d) Convert the worksheet to show formulas.

(e) Set the page orientation to landscape.

(f) Save the workbook.

TASK 3

On a new worksheet:

(a)   Name the new worksheet 'Currency Conversion'.

(b)   Return to the 'Data' worksheet and Auto-Filter the data.

(c)   Filter by sales person 'Monty Video'.

(d)   Copy the result and paste it into Cell A1 in the currency conversion worksheet.

(e)   Return to the Data worksheet and remove the 'Monty Video' filter.

(f)   Save the workbook.

TASK 4

On the 'Currency Conversion' worksheet:

(a)   Insert 3 rows at the top of the worksheet.

(b)   In Cell D1, type 'Conversion Rate' and make the font bold and underline the text. Format D1 to Right Justified.

(c)   Format Cell E1 to number to 2 decimal places and type 0.84.

(d)   Make the font bold in cells A4:I4.

(e)   In Cell E5:E26 create a formula that converts the content of Cell D5:D26 to GBP (£) by multiplying by the conversion rate in Cell E1. Use absolute referencing where necessary.

(f)   The sales price is 20% more than the cost price £. In cells F5:F26 use a formula to calculate the sales price.

(g)   Copy cells A4:I26 from the 'Currency conversion' worksheet and paste special, to include the values and number formatting, into a new worksheet and rename the new worksheet as 'Profit Calculation'.

(h)   Return to the 'Currency conversion' worksheet and show formulas. Auto fit the column widths.

(i)   Set the page orientation to landscape.

(j)   Save the workbook.

TASK 5

On the 'Profit Calculation' worksheet:

(a)   In Cells J1, K1 and L1 create 3 new headings of 'Total Cost', 'Total Revenue' and 'Profit'. Make all the column heading bold.

(b)   In Cell J2:J23 create a formula that calculates the total cost (Cost price in £ multiplied by Sales Quantity)

(c)   In Cell K2:K23 create a formula that calculates the total revenue (Sales Price multiplied by Sales Quantity.

(d)   In Cell L2:L23 create a formula that calculates profit (Total Revenue – Total Cost).

(e)   In Cells J25:L25 use a function to calculate the average cost, average revenue and the average profit. Add the heading 'Averages' in cell I25.

(f)   In Cells J26:L26 use a function to calculate the largest number in each of the data sets. Add the heading 'Largest' in cell I26.

(g)   In Cells J27:L27 use a function to calculate the smallest number in each of the data sets. Add the heading 'Smallest' in cell I27.

(h)   Show formulas and auto-fit column widths.

(i)   Set the page orientation to landscape, and move the page break to the left of column I.

(j)   Save the workbook.

TASK 6

On the 'Data' worksheet:

(a)   Using the data create a Pivot Table in a new worksheet that shows the quantity of each individual model sold by each salesperson. The model should be the columns and the salesperson the rows.

(b)   Rename the worksheet 'Pivot' and move it to the right of the 'Profit Calculation' sheet.

(c)   Remove Grand Totals for Rows and Columns.

(d)   Create a Pivot Chart and locate it on the Pivot worksheet. The type of chart should be a Clustered Column Chart. Add the title 'Sales Quantity' to the chart.

(e)   Add Customer as a Filter.

(f)   Save the workbook.

TASK 7

On a new worksheet:

(a)   Name the new worksheet 'Product Lookup'.

(b)   In cell A2 type 'Product Code', in cell A6 type 'Inventory levels' and in cell A9 type 'Sales quantity'. Fit the contents to the cell.

(c)   In cell B2 create a list of product codes from the 'Data' worksheet using Data Validation. Pick the product code WM4369.

(d)   In cell B6 create a VLOOKUP to look up the product code in Cell B2 in the 'Data' worksheet and return the quantity. The VLOOKUP should be set to look for only exact matches.

(e)   In cell B9 create a VLOOKUP to look up the product code in Cell B2 in the 'Data' worksheet and return the sales quantity. The VLOOKUP should be set to look for only exact matches.

(f)   In Cell B12, use an IF function that produces the word "Re-order" if the value in Cell B9 is greater than the value in Cell B6 but leaves it blank if not.

(g)   In cell C12, use an IF function that calculates the difference between the inventory levels and the sales quantity if "Re-order" appears in B12 but leaves it blank if not.

(h)   Set page orientation to landscape.

(i)   Save the workbook.

SCENARIO 2

BETTABAKE

You work for a small bakery. They are very good at making cakes but not very good at doing their budgets. They are constantly running out of ingredients because they do not predict accurately what cakes they are going to make that day.

Four of the cakes the bakery produces are:

The Whirl

Splash

Butterbun

Chocco

Ingredient requirements for each product are:

Cake	Eggs	Flour	Sugar	Butter	Cream
The Whirl	1	50g	35g	28g	12g
Splash	1.5	30g	18g	22g	10g
Butterbun	2	65g	27g	24g	0
Chocco	1	55g	30g	21g	0

The following information is also available with regards to costs:

Ingredient	Quantity	Total cost
Eggs	12	£1.50
Flour	200g	£1.80
Sugar	200g	£2.20
Butter	1000g	£6.00
Cream	300g	£2.50

Required:

The Production Manager wants you to prepare a spreadsheet workbook that will help her with her budgets.

TASK 1

On the 'Budget data' worksheet:

(a)   In cells D10:D14 insert a formula to calculate the cost per unit in a pack. Make sure the cells are formatted to Currency £ and 4 decimal places.

On the 'Cost per cake' worksheet:

(b)   Using the 'Ingredients' and the 'Cost per unit' data on the 'Budget data' worksheet use formulas in cells B2 to F5 to calculate the total cost of each ingredient for each cake. Give consideration to absolute and relative referencing.

(c)   Use a function to calculate the total cost per cake.

(d)   Format all cells as currency £ to 3 decimal places.

(e)   Show formulas and auto-fit column widths.

(f)   Set the page orientation to landscape.

(g)   Save your work as 'Bettabake'.

TASK 2

On the 'Budget' worksheet:

(a)   Insert the quantities in B2:B5 as:

The Whirl	35
Splash	9
Butterbun	15
Chocco	24

(b)   In cells C2:G5 create a formula that calculates the quantity of ingredients required to manufacture the number of cakes entered in Column B. This will use the 'Budget data' worksheet. Use absolute referencing where necessary.

(c)   Use a function to calculate the totals in cells C6:G6.

(d)   Format the values in the table to number with no decimal places.

(e)   In cells C7:G7 calculate the purchase quantities for each ingredient. Eggs are purchased in boxes of 360 all other ingredients are purchased by the kg (1,000g). Use a formula that will round the purchase quantity up to the nearest whole box or kg.

(f)   Save the workbook.

TASK 3

On the 'Budget' worksheet:

(a)   Insert the following selling prices into cells C14:C17

Cake	£
The Whirl	0.90
Splash	1.20
Butterbun	1.10
Chocco	1.50

(b)   Use a VLOOKUP to look up the cost price from the 'Cost per Cake' worksheet in cells B14:B17.

(c)   Use a function in cells D14:D17 to calculate profit that rounds the answer to 2 decimal places.

(d)   Use conditional formatting to turn any cells in the profit column red where a product is loss making.

(e)   Auto-fit to columns and set orientation to landscape.

(f)   Save your work.

TASK 4

On the 'Whirl' worksheet:

(a)   Your manager wants to calculate the future possible sales amounts for The Whirl. On the 'Whirl' worksheet produce a scatter graph for weeks 1 to 10 with a line of best fit showing the trend on the sales.

(b)   Use the Forecast function to predict the sales for weeks 11 and 12 (cells B12 and B13). Round the answers down to the nearest whole cake.

(c)   Save your work.

TASK 5

On the 'Budget' worksheet:

(a)   Using What-if analysis calculate what the selling price would need to be for the Butterbun to make a total profit of £3.00

(b)   **BEFORE** you click OK take a screen shot of the What-if analysis and paste it into a new worksheet. Name the worksheet 'Screenshot'.

(c)   Save your work.

SCENARIO 3

CRAZY CARS

You work as a payroll assistant for a car sales company called Crazy Cars.

Required:

TASK 1

On the 'Employee Information' worksheet:

(a)   Place the TODAY function in Cell B10.

(b)   In column C use a formula to calculate the number of days each employee has worked for Crazy Cars with reference to the TODAY function in Cell B10. Use absolute and relative referencing where appropriate. Change the format of these cells to general so the number of days is shown rather than the date.

(c)   In column D use a function to convert the number of days into years, rounding down to the nearest whole year.

(d)   Show formulas and auto-fit column widths.

(e)   Save your work as 'Crazy Cars'.

TASK 2

On the 'Basic Pay' worksheet:

The basic wage is dependent on the number of full years each employee has worked for the business.

An employee's starting rate (for the first 12 months) is £160 per week.

The basic rate per week increases by 10% for each full year of employment up to a maximum of 5 years.

(a)   Using the information above calculate the weekly pay for an employee at the company based on 0 to 25 years of employment.

(b)   Format the basic wage to pounds and pence.

(c)   Save your work.

TASK 3

The sales team are paid a basic wage plus commission for the cars that they sell.

Each employee receives 5% of the profit they have earned from each car they have sold that week.

Any cars sold at a loss must be highlighted for the Finance Manager.

On the 'Car Sales Information' worksheet:

(a)   In column E use a formula to calculate the profit (sales less cost) made for each vehicle. Add a suitable title in cell E1.

(b)   Using an IF function, in column F calculate the amount of commission earned on each vehicle. If the car has been sold at a loss, then "none" should appear in the cell. Add a suitable title in cell F1.

(c)   All monetary values should be formatted to currency (£) to 2 decimal places.

(d)   In column E use conditional formatting to identify the value of any losses. The cell fill should turn red.

(e)   Auto-fit column widths.

(f)   Save your work.

TASK 4

Using the 'Car Sales Information' worksheet:

(a)   Create a pivot table in a new worksheet that shows the total commission earned by each salesperson (columns) per make of car (rows).

(b)   Format the values in the pivot table as currency £ to 2 decimal places.

(c)   Name the pivot table worksheet as 'Pivot'.

(d)   Move the 'Pivot' worksheet to the right of the 'Car Sales Information' worksheet.

(e)   Save your work.

TASK 5

On the 'Total Pay' worksheet:

(a)   Show the following information:

   (ii)   In column B, use a VLOOKUP from the 'Employee Information' worksheet to extract the number of years each employee has been employed.

   (iii)   In column C, use a VLOOKUP from the 'Basic Pay' worksheet, to calculate the applicable basic weekly pay for each employee.

   (iv)   In column D, use a HLOOKUP from the 'Pivot' worksheet, enter the commission earned per employee.

   (v)   In cell D10 use a function to determine the average commission earned.

   (vi)   Any member of staff who earns more than the average commission each week receives an extra £100 bonus. In column E use an IF statement that calculate any bonus.

   (vii)   In column F, using the Sum function – calculate the total pay for each employee for the week and the total wages the company is paying that week.

   (viii)   Format all monetary amounts to pounds and pence.

   (ix)   Show formulas and auto-fit column widths.

(b)   Save your work.

TASK 6

The Finance Director wants to see how each sales person has contributed to the total commission earned.

(a)   Create a pie chart using the 'Total Pay' worksheet to show each employees commission as a proportion of the total commission.

(b)   Give the pie chart a suitable title and add percentage labels to the chart.

(c)   Move the pie chart to a new worksheet called 'Pie chart' and move the sheet to the right of the 'Total Pay' worksheet.

(d)   Save your work.

SCENARIO 4

GOODTIME TRAVEL

Goodtime Travel is a firm of Travel Agents that specialises in long haul package holidays. It buys the flights and hotel rooms in bulk from the airlines and hotels. It is a reputable firm and gets most of its custom from customers who have used its service before.

Required:

TASK 1

Customers can receive discounts off their holidays. A discount will only be given if a customer has booked a previous holiday with Goodtime Travel. A discount is given of 2p per mile flown on the previous holiday.

This discount is then deducted from the price of the current holiday. However, the Finance Director is considering adapting the discount rates so that they are different for each destination. Details of the miles travelled for each destination are given on the Discounts worksheet.

On the 'Discounts' worksheet:

(a)   In Column C use a formula to calculate the discount for a particular destination, use absolute referencing where appropriate.

(b)   Format the discount column as currency (£) to 2 decimal places.

(c)   Show formulas and auto-fit column widths.

On the 'Weekly Sales' worksheet:

(d)   In the Discount column (column F) use a VLOOKUP from the 'Discounts' worksheet to calculate any applicable discounts.

(e)   In the column G, use a formula to calculate the amount owing for each booking deducting any discounts for repeat customers.

(f)   Format the values to £ currency to 2 decimal places in columns F and G.

(g)   Set the orientation to landscape and fit the data to one page.

(h)   Save the workbook as 'Goodtime Travel'.

TASK 2

Goodtime Travel has recently invested in a marketing campaign to try and encourage new customers to use its service. The Marketing Manager has said that the campaign will be viewed as a success if at least 40% of income each week is generated from new customers.

On the 'Weekly sales' worksheet:

(a)   Create a pivot table in a new worksheet to show how much revenue has been generated from new customers compared to existing customers (columns) for the different destinations (rows).

(b)   Call this worksheet 'Pivot' and move it to the right of the 'Weekly sales' worksheet.

(c)   In cell G15 on the 'Pivot' worksheet create an expression to calculate the total % of income generated from new customers. The answer should be formatted as percentage and 2 decimal places. In cell F15 add the title "% new customers" and fit the content to the cell.

(d)   In cell H15 use an IF function for the Marketing Director to determine whether the campaign was a success. "Successful" should appear if more than 40% of the income is generated from new customers and "Unsuccessful" if less than 40% of the income is generated from new customers. Format the outcome of the IF formula by making it bold, and enlarging the text to font size 16.

(e)   Save the workbook.

TASK 3

The Finance Director is considering changing the discount on offer per mile for repeat customers. He wants the discount amounts for the following destinations changed to:

Destination	New Discount	Currently
Sydney	£250.00	£424.00
Fiji	£300.00	£404.36

On the 'What If Analysis' worksheet:

(a)   Copy all the discount information from the 'Discount' worksheet and paste it into the 'What if Analysis' worksheet.

(b)   Using What If Analysis – Goal Seek, calculate what the revised discount rate per mile needs to be to reduce the discount offered for Sydney. Copy and 'paste–special values' the result to cell D20. Provide a suitable heading in A20. Reset the original discount rate per mile to 2p.

(c)   Using What If Analysis – Goal Seek, calculate what the revised discount rate per mile needs to be to reduce the discount offered for Fiji. Copy and 'paste–special values' the result to cell D22. Provide a suitable heading in A22. Reset the original discount rate per mile to 2p.

(d)   Show formulas, auto-fit column width and save your work.

(e)   Save the workbook.

SCENARIO 5

STAR TICKETS

You work for Star Tickets, a small company selling tickets for music concerts.

Star Tickets have asked you to help them create a spreadsheet to help manage their ticket sales. They have given you the details for today's sales:

Artist	Day of concert	Customer payment		Ticket seller
		Sales price	Amount paid	
Nancy Arbuckle	Saturday	£30	£10	Jane
Other Way	Tuesday	£60	£60	Mark
Down Stream	Wednesday	£90	£90	Mark
Upright Legs	Friday	£80	£80	Karen
Other Way	Tuesday	£30	£15	Jane
Nancy Arbuckle	Saturday	£45	£45	Mark
Down Stream	Friday	£34	£34	Jane

TASK 1

The 'Data' worksheet contains lists of artists, sellers and the various discounts to be used to calculate ticket prices on the 'Ticket Sales' worksheet.

Star Tickets buys tickets from concert venues to sell them on to customers. The face value of the tickets is £50, but Star Tickets receives discounts depending on which day the concert takes place.

On the 'Data' worksheet:

(a)   Use a formula in cells C2:C8 to calculate the discounted price for each day.

(b)   Protect the worksheet so that users are only able to enter data into Cells D2:E8

On the 'Ticket sales' worksheet:

(c)   Use Data Validation to create drop down lists for Artist; Day of Week; Ticket Seller in columns A, B and C respectively. You will need to copy the data validation down each column to row 8. Insert the information for today's sales from the table in the scenario.

(d)   In the purchase price column, create a VLOOKUP that selects the correct discounted purchase price based on the day of the week.

(e)   Enter the data from the scenario for the sales price and amount paid.

(f)   In the amount outstanding column create a formula that takes the amount paid from the sales price.

(g)   In the profit/loss column create a formula that calculates the profit or a loss based on sales price less purchase price.

Star Tickets sales staff aim to sell each ticket for as much as possible; if they sell a ticket for more than its purchase price they receive a bonus.

(h)   In the bonus payable? column, use an IF function to determine whether a bonus is due. If a bonus is due the function should return "Yes" if not, then the function should return "No".

(i)   Set all monetary amounts on the 'Ticket Sales' worksheet to currency £ and 2 decimal places.

(j)   Save the workbook as 'Star Tickets'.

TASK 2

On the 'Ticket sales' worksheet:

(a)   Use conditional formatting to fill cells red in the profit/loss column where a loss has been made.

(b)   In cell A10 label the row "Totals". Use a function to calculate the totals below the sales price and the amount outstanding column. Use single line border at the top of these cells and double line border at the bottom of the cells.

Customers can pay in instalments, although management have said that at the end of each day the total outstanding balance owed by all customers cannot be greater than 10% of the total sales generated that day.

(c)   In Cell G15 create a formula to determine how much of the sales are outstanding as a percentage of total sales made. Format as percentage and 2 decimal places. Provide a suitable bold heading in cell F15 and right align the heading.

(d)   In cell H15 create an IF Function that determines whether the percentage would be acceptable to management. The function should return either "OK" or "Not Acceptable".

(e)   Set orientation to landscape, show formulas, auto-fit column width and fit the data to one page

(f)   Save the workbook.

TASK 3

Management are also keen to identify any unpopular artists whose tickets are not making a profit for the company.

(a)   Using the data on the 'Ticket sales' worksheet create a pivot table in a new worksheet to show how much profit each ticket seller has made (columns), by Artist (rows).

(b)   Rename the worksheet 'Pivot' and move it to the right of the 'Ticket Sales' worksheet.

(c)   Use conditional formatting to highlight the cells yellow in the pivot table where a loss has been made.

(d)   Save the workbook.

Section 2

MOCK ASSESSMENT 1 – QUESTIONS

You will be required to open an Excel spreadsheet called Laura that contains data you require for this assessment. The spreadsheet can be found on MyKaplan. The spreadsheet will need to be downloaded and saved before starting the tasks.

You MUST save your work at regular intervals during this assessment to prevent you losing work.

Laura's Luggage manufactures and sells luggage to retailers, online and through their own factory outlet.

The company wishes to work out how well it has been performing and has asked you to assist by building a spreadsheet to calculate costs, revenue and profits for the first six months of 2024.

TASK 1

On the 'Volumes' worksheet:

(a)   Use formulae or functions to calculate the following:

- The closing inventory for each month (closing inventory is calculated as opening Inventory plus production volume minus sales volume)

- The opening inventory for each month by bringing forward the closing inventory from the previous month

- The cost of sales volume for each month (cost of sales is calculated as opening inventory plus production volume minus closing inventory)

- The total production volume (cell D10) for the first six months of 2024 and the total sales volume (cell B10) for the first 6 months of 2024. Add the title 'Total' in A10.

(b)   Format the table of data in the following way:

- The volume figures in your table of data should be set to number to zero decimal places with a 1000 separator.

- The column headings, using bold, Arial, font size 11 and wrapped over two lines to reduce column width.

On the 'Costs and sales prices' worksheet:

The table below shows the way in which the company calculated cost and sales prices during 2024.

Quarter	Cost per item	Sales price
1 (Jan – Mar)	£48.50	Cost + 23%
2 (Apr – Jun)	4% increase from Q1	Cost + 23%
3 (Jul – Sept)	6% increase from Q1	Cost + 23%
4 (Oct – Dec)	5% increase from Q1	Cost + 25%

(c)   Using the data above use formulae to complete cells B4:C9. Use a function to round the values to 2 decimal places.

(d)   Format the values to currency.

(e)   Save the workbook 'Laura's Luggage'.

TASK 2

On the 'Volumes' worksheet:

(a)   Use a formula and a VLOOKUP to convert the sales volumes to monetary values in the 'Profits and Margins for 2024' table cells B15:B20. The VLOOKUP should look up the month and return the sales price per item from the Costs and sales prices worksheet. Total this column

(b)   Use a formula and a VLOOKUP to convert the Cost of sales volumes to monetary values in the 'Profits and Margins for 2024' table cells C15:C20. The VLOOKUP should look up the month and return the cost per item from the Costs and sales prices worksheet.

(c)   In cells F15 to I20 use formulae to calculate gross and net profit figures. To do this you will need to either use formulae or input data as per the following instructions:

    1   Gross profit is calculated as sales revenue minus the cost of sales.

    2   Expenses are £63,000 in Quarter 1 rising by 5% in each successive quarter.

    3   Net profit is calculated as gross profit minus expenses.

(d)   Total the gross profit and net profit columns.

(e)   In cells G15:H20 you are going to use formulae to calculate the gross profit and net profit margins:

    1   Gross profit margin is gross profit as a percentage of sales revenue.

    2   Net profit margin is net profit as a percentage of sales revenue.

(f)   Format the table in the following way:

    1   All column totals should be in bold.

    2   Format all monetary cells to currency £ to two decimal places.

    3   Percentages should be to two decimal places.

(g)   Rename the worksheet 'Lugg001'.

Management would like the net profit margin to be greater than 15% each month.

(h) Use an IF statement in cells I15:I20 to show management which months agree with the statement above. Make "Yes" appear in the cell if it does agree or "No" if it does not agree.

(i) Save the workbook.

TASK 3

You have been asked to investigate different aspects of the budget for 2024.

Firstly, you need to review the costs for the first quarter of 2024 (January, February and March) which were entered onto the computer by your line manager.

Using the 'PC2024' worksheet:

(a) Format the column headers with bold text ensuring column widths and row heights are suitable for the contents. Wrap text across 2 lines if required.

(b) Format all the dates as dd/mm/yyyy, make amendments as required so that all dates are in the required format. Sort the data by date, in ascending order. Ensure that only the correct information is used for the quarter by deleting the irrelevant information.

(c) You have discovered additional materials and overheads not included in the spreadsheet. Insert rows and/or columns at the correct date and enter the following costs. Ensure the row total calculates correctly and it must remain as the last column on the worksheet.

• Materials 7th February	£112,077.80
• Materials 16 Jan 24	£179,440.10
• 5th Jan, Overheads	£14,800
• 5th Feb, Overheads	£12,300
• 5th March, Overheads	£11,100

(d) Total all the columns.

(e) Format all numerical cells as £ currency and round to two decimal places.

(f) Under the total in column D, use a function to calculate the average material cost.

(g) Use conditional formatting to highlight cells in which the material values exceed the average figure for materials. The conditional formatting should change the cell fill to red and the text to white and bold.

(h) Produce a pie chart of the column totals. Ensure the legend contains the column header names and that the chart has a suitable title. The pie chart should show percentages on the outside of the circle.

(i) Ensure all of the information is displayed in a way that could be printed on one A4 page.

(j) Save the workbook.

TASK 4

The managers have some queries concerning bag sales.

You have been asked to identify the most popular type of bag sold and the best performing sales method, (Internet, Factory Shop or Retail) from the given information of each type of sale for each month.

Using the 'LLData' worksheet:

(a)   There has been an error in inputting; Internet sales have been recorded both as 'Internet' and 'Online'. Replace all instances of 'Online' with 'Internet'. Take a screenshot of the Find and replace wizard before you click OK and paste the screenshot into a new worksheet. Call this new worksheet 'Screenshot'.

(b)   Create a pivot table. The pivot table should be placed to the right of the data set starting in cell H1. Use the pivot table to show the total quantity (values) of each type of bag sold (rows) for each sales outlet (columns).

(c)   Add a filter for the month.

(d)   Copy the data in columns A:D and paste into a new worksheet.   Call this worksheet 'Subtotals'.

(e)   Save the workbook.

TASK 5

Using the 'Subtotals' worksheet:

(a)   Sort the data by Sales outlet, then by Bag type.

(b)   Create subtotals for Sales outlet, summing on quantity sold.

(c)   Create a further subtotal for Bag type, summing on quantity sold.

(d)   Show the Bag type and Sales outlet totals only on the worksheet.

(e)   Save the workbook.

Section 3

MOCK ASSESSMENT 2 – QUESTIONS

You will be required to open an Excel spreadsheet called HVN&Co that contains data you require for this assessment. The spreadsheet can be found on MyKaplan. The spreadsheet will need to be downloaded and saved before starting the tasks.

You MUST save your work at regular intervals during this assessment to prevent you losing work.

You are Steve Jones, a part-qualified accounting technician. You work for HVN & Co, a business which manufactures and sells guitar effects pedals. HVN & Co is owned and run by Helen and Vincent Ng in partnership.

You cover all aspects of bookkeeping and accountant for the business.

TASK 1

HVN & Co have introduced a new accounting system and are currently running both systems in parallel as part of the changeover process. Unfortunately, the two systems are showing different sales figures, which is causing some alarm. You have been asked to complete the quarterly sales spreadsheet for the three months ended 31 March 20X7 which has been produced by going back to copies of the original sales invoices.

Today's date is 15 April 20X7.

On the 'Invoices' worksheet:

(a)   Check for and remove any duplicates in the invoices. If there were any duplicates, enter the number found in I1. Remove the duplicates.

(b)   Use a vlookup function on the 'Item No' data to calculate the net sales using information from the 'Price List' worksheet (net sales equals the selling price per item multiplied by the quantity sold).

(c)   Use absolute referencing to calculate the gross sales value of each invoice using the VAT figure provided in cell H1 (gross sales value equals the net sales plus the VAT).

(d)   Make sure all the contents of every cell can be seen.

(e)   Save the workbook as 'HVN&Co'.

TASK 2

On the 'Invoices' worksheet:

(a)   Insert a pivot chart (clustered column) and pivot table into a new worksheet showing the net sales (values) in each of the three months from January to March (rows). Add the channel as a filter and select the Amazon channel. Name this worksheet 'Amazon Sales'.

On the 'Amazon Sales' worksheet:

(b)   Manually format the chart series to show best sales for the period in black and worst sales in red

(c)   Add a chart title 'Amazon Sales'

(d)   Make sure the legend is clearly visible

(e)   Add a linear trend line, making it dashed and colour it red

(f)   Change the filter on your pivot table to include all channels

(g)   Use your pivot table to determine the total sales for each month through all channels. Copy the values of these into the relevant cells in the worksheet 'Forecast'

(h)   Set your pivot table back to just Amazon sales before saving.

(i)   Save the workbook

On the 'Forecast' worksheet:

(j)   Use the FORECAST function to predict the sales for the next three months

(k)   Save the workbook.

TASK 3

On the 'Invoices' worksheet:

(a)   Sort the data to enable the data to be subtotalled.

(b)   Create subtotals for Type, summing on quantity sold.

(c)   Create a further subtotal for Channel, summing on quantity sold.

(d)   Save the workbook.

TASK 4

On the 'HVN1' worksheet:

You are helping to prepare the final accounts for HVN & Co for the year ended 31 December 20X7. Partners may take drawings (money) out of the business but get charged interest at 1% per month if the cumulative drawings figure exceeds £25,000. This is calculated on the month-end cumulative balance.

(a)   Format all headings to have bold size 12 font.

(b)   Merge and centre the partners' names over their respective columns. Align the month column, including the heading, to the left. Align the other columns, including the category headers, to the right.

(c)   Calculate the cumulative position of each partner for each month.

(d)   Use an IF statement to calculate the interest on drawings for each partner for each month. If there is no interest the cell should contain 0 (number zero).

(e)   In Row 19 total each of the columns D and G.

(f)   Format the range of figures in cells B6:G18 in currency with the thousand separator and zero decimal places (e.g. £3,200).

(g)   Format the table so there is an outside border around Helen's data and another around Vincent's data.

(h)   Save the workbook.

On the 'What-if' worksheet

Helen asks you what figure for 'profit for the year' would need to be if her 'profit share' were to be £350,000. Assume all other data is uncharged.

(i)   Use Goal Seek analysis to answer Helen's question. Take a screenshot of the Goal Seek wizard and paste it on to the 'What-if' worksheet starting in cell H1.

(j)   Save the workbook.

TASK 5

On 1 September 20X7 HVN & Co started selling a new 'chorus' pedal.

The original budget for the quarter to 31 December 20X7 is in the 'Original Budget' worksheet of the provided spreadsheet. The original plan was to sell 150 per month at a price of £120 each, but actual sales for the period amounted to 165 units at the lower price of £118.

Vincent has already input some formulae and functions into the 'original budget' worksheet.

On the 'original budget' worksheet:

(a)   The original plan was to produce and sell 150 per month but actual production and sales for the period amounted to 165 units. In cell D1 calculate the percentage (%) increase in the number of units sold. Format cell D1 as 'Percentage'.

(b)   The actual revenue and costs for the quarter are shown in the worksheet headed 'Actual results'. Use 'copy' and 'paste link' to insert these from the source worksheet into the correct positions in column E of the 'Original Budget' worksheet.

(c)   Use conditional formatting in column F to show whether variances are "Favourable" (a positive value) or "Adverse" (a negative value). Turn the cell green if favourable and red if adverse.

(d)   Save the workbook.

Section 4

ANSWERS TO PRACTICE SCENARIOS AND MOCK EXAMS

The answers to the scenarios and mocks can be found as spreadsheet files on your MyKaplan account (together with the text and word files required).

Please go to www.mykaplan.co.uk and login using your username and password.